This book belongs to
_____

Copyright © 2025 Grow Grit Press LLC. All rights reserved. No part of this book may be reproduced in any form without permission in writing from the publisher. Please send bulk order requests to info@ninjalifehacks.tv

Paperback ISBN: 979-8-89614-106-8
Hardcover ISBN: 979-8-89614-108-2
eBook ISBN: 979-8-89614-107-5

Printed and bound in the USA.
NinjaLifeHacks.tv

CALM COW

By
Mary Nhin

SOCIAL SUPERHEROES

Calm Cow? Oh, not quite yet!
She huffed, she puffed, she'd often fret.
Her tail swished fast, her hooves hit ground,
her mind raced wild, her mood spun round!

One day, while munching grass so sweet,
her mind raced fast—she stomped her feet!
"Too much noise! Too much to do!"
She paced around and mooed and mooed!

Oh boy! Here we go again.

She stomped past Focused Fox, hiding near the hay.
Fox muttered, "Would you like to try a new way?"
"When life feels wild and thoughts won't slow,
try yoga moves—just breathe and flow!"

"Yoga? Me?" Cow raised a brow.
"I don't bend—I'm just a cow!"
But Fox just grinned and struck a pose.
"Let's start real simple—touch your toes!"

"Stretch down slow, let your head hang light,
breathe in deep—it feels just right."
Cow bent low—her tail swayed too,
and guess what? She felt brand new!

"Next," said Fox, "is Cow Pose—see?
This one's named for you AND me!"
Cow arched her back, stretched high, stretched low,
then let a peaceful "moo" echo.

"Now round your back like Cat Pose here.
Breathe in, breathe out, the sky is clear!"
Cow curved up high, her tail went swish.
She felt much lighter—whoa, what's this?!

She's getting it!

"Let's try one more!" Fox said with cheer,
"Plant your hooves and lift your rear!"
Cow tipped forward, tail to sky,
"Whoa! I feel so calm—oh my!"

"Last one, Cow! Now stand up tall,
Tree Pose helps you not to fall!"
Cow lifted one hoof and wobbled wide.
Then found her balance as she stood with pride!

Cow took a breath, slow and deep.
Her body felt light, her mind at peace.
"Fox, this worked! I'm calm—hooray!
Let's do this every single day."

Now Cow, once rushed and full of woe,
knows how to breathe, stretch, and flow.
If stress sneaks in, she strikes a pose,
and *just like that*, her worry goes!

So if your mind feels much too tight,
or worries keep you up at night,
Try some yoga, just like Cow.
Breathe in, breathe out... you'll feel good now!

Stand up tall, give it a go!
Stretch, relax, and find your flow.
A calm, cool mind will always show
when you breathe, stretch, and take it slow.

Calm Cow's Yoga & Breath Adventure: Activity Page

Draw Calm Cow!

Draw Calm Cow in your favorite yoga pose! Is she doing Tree Pose? Downward Dog? Add Fox or another silly animal friend too!

Finish the Sentence

When I feel stressed like Calm Cow, I can…

1. Take a deep breath and _____.
2. Stretch like a _____ and hold it for 10 seconds.
3. Say something kind to myself like, "_____."

Try It Yourself: Cow's Yoga Challenge!

Stand up and try these 3 moves Calm Cow learned:

- ✅ Forward Fold – Bend down and let your arms dangle
- ✅ Cow Pose – Arch your back and say "Mooooo!"
- ✅ Tree Pose – Lift one leg and try to balance!

How did you feel after trying them? Circle one:

🙂 Calm   😐 Okay   😶 Wobbly   😲 Silly   😴 Sleepy

Check out the Calm Cow Lesson Plans at www.ninjalifehacks.tv

 @marynhin   @officialninjalifehacks   Ninja Life Hacks
#NinjaLifeHacks

 Mary Nhin   Ninja Life Hacks   @officialninjalifehacks

SOCIAL SUPERHEROES

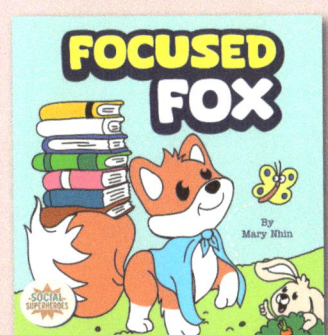   

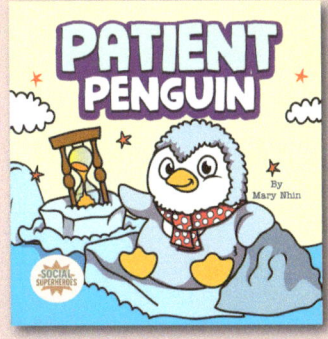 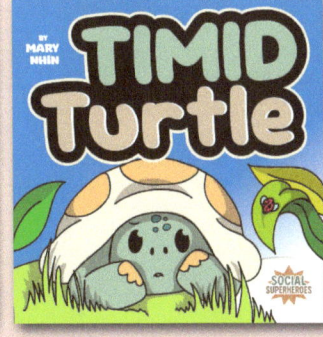 

www.ingramcontent.com/pod-product-compliance
Lightning Source LLC
LaVergne TN
LVHW070435070526
838199LV00015B/513